The HARRISON & DUNN STORY

A HISTORY AND MEMOIR

By MICHAEL LEE

Additional material by
Andrew Lee and Harold Bluff

Content transcribed by Sue Lord
Edited by Christopher Birks
Cover design and book layout by Alex Birks

This edition published 2025

First amended version 2026
Published by The Harrison & Dunn Story

All images marked † are the property of Andrew Lee

All images except otherwise indicated by † or within the image caption are the property of Sheila Lee

Cover design, book design and typeset by Alex Birks
www.alexbirks.co.uk

Proofreading services provided by Siân Smith of Sian Smith Editorial
www.siansmitheditorial.co.uk

Enquiries regarding this publication should be made to the editor,
Christopher Birks
christopher@christopherbirks.co.uk

ISBN 978-1-0369-1141-6

I dedicate this book to my wife, Sheila, who I think was the true, hard-working ironmonger; a constant companion to me, both in work and family.

Michael Lee

CONTENTS

LIST OF FIGURES

EDITOR'S PREFACE

My intention here in presenting Michael Lee's *The Harrison & Dunn Story* is to replicate and honour Lee's exact words as much as possible. Lee dictated his content, and thus *The Story* can – and should – be considered an invaluable piece of oral history. To that end, I have endeavoured to preserve the words, syntax, and rhythm of Lee's speech. The only edits I have made (made, I might add, with reticence) are simply when absolutely required for comprehension and to thematically arrange Lee's content as presented in this book.

In order to enhance *The Story's* status as a piece of oral history – a history relevant to any social, economic, or political history of the United Kingdom (more specifically, of England, and more specifically still, of Stamford, Lincolnshire, and its surrounding towns and villages) – there has been no attempt made to confirm or challenge any of the dates, events, or claims recorded here by Lee. In future editions, one would like to present expansions, corroborations, or even refutations alongside Lee's work; however, that is not the intention or spirit of this edition.

Figure 1: Map of Stamford town centre, showing locations of Harrison & Dunn and Duncomb & Co. Ltd premises (ArcGIS Online, hosted by Esri Community Maps Contributors, Esri UK, Esri, TomTom, Garmin, Foursquare, GeoTechnologies, Inc, METI/NASA, USGS, 2025).

MAP

▲ HARRISON & DUNN
9, 10 & 11 All Saints' Street

● HARRISON & DUNN
3 All Saints' Street

■ DUNCOMB & CO. LTD
5-6 High Street

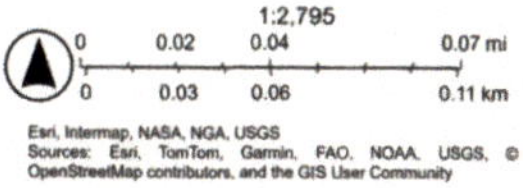

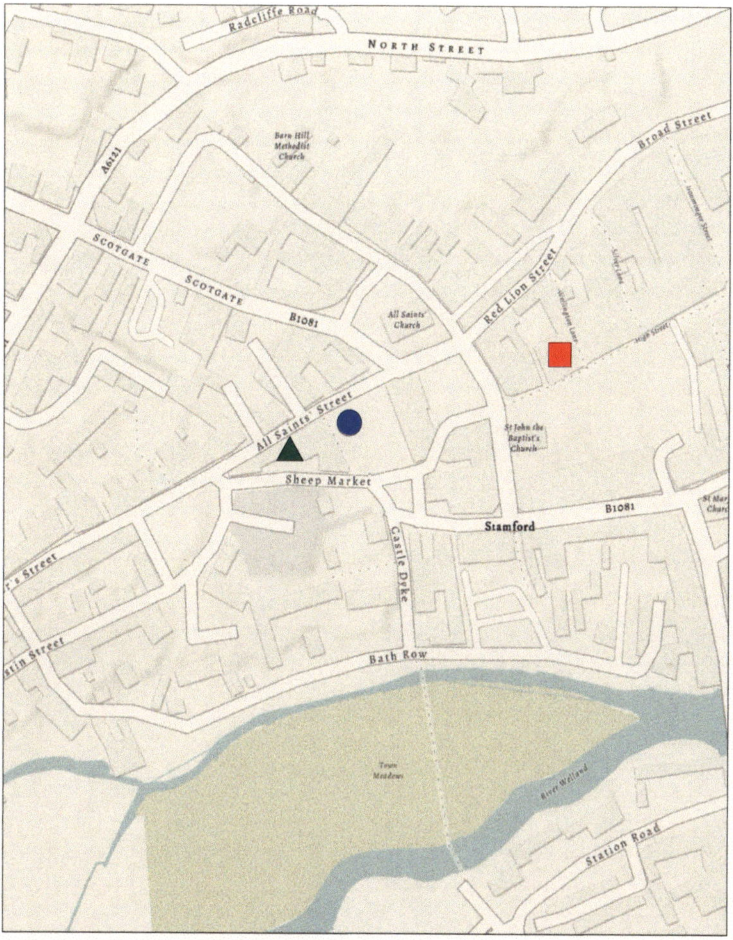

CHAPTER 1

THE HARRISON & DUNN STORY

THE BEGINNING OF A PARTNERSHIP

This is the story of Harrison & Dunn, ironmonger, and how, as it approaches its 100th year of trading, it has survived in a changing world. It started trading on the 23rd of May 1930, in a small premises at 10 All Saints' Street in Stamford, Lincolnshire. But I should like to begin its story with the history of how the two partners came to form a business together in the first place.

MR HARRISON, MR DUNCOMB, AND MR DUNN

Mr William Harrison was born some eight miles north of Stamford in the small village of Clipsham (an area well known for its stone quarries). He was born in the Victorian era, in the year 1891. At the age of thirteen, the family moved to Vine Street in Stamford. He was successful in obtaining an apprenticeship to learn the trade of an ironmonger with Mr Tommy Duncomb, the proprietor of a very large and successful shop at 5 High Street, Stamford.

Mr T.S. Duncomb – a Stamford man born and bred – had purchased this business in 1888 from a Mr John Britton, an ironmonger who had been trading in Stamford for many years (see *Figure 2*). In 1904, at the time when Mr Harrison began working for Mr Duncomb, the shop had been very much improved and enlarged. It was now joined to 6 High Street, with showrooms on the first floor (see *Figures 3–4*). This was a time when local business owners sought and often achieved prominent positions in local government, and Mr Duncomb was no exception: he was at this time a local councillor with the Stamford Borough Council, and by 1908 would be mayor and chief magistrate.

Figure 2†: T.S. Duncomb, ironmonger, at 5 High Street, Stamford, c.1888–1894. Mr T.S. Duncomb is standing second from the right. The advert below the window is for washing machines and mangles; on the front step there are paraffin heaters and cookers, with horse hames hanging above; hanging from the fascia are copper and tin plate kettles (made in the shop's workshop), and on top are hand lawnmowers, garden pots, hand pressure sprays, and farm hay rakes; in the shop windows there is a fireplace, piles of chests and cases, pots, china, and tools.

Figure 3†: T.S. Duncomb, ironmonger, at 5–6 High Street (on the left), Stamford, c.1896.

Figure 4†: T.S. Duncomb, ironmonger, at 5–6 High Street, Stamford, 1920s.

In 1910, as Mr Harrison was completing his apprenticeship, Mr Albert Dunn was born. His family home was 6 New Street, not far from that of his future business partner on Vine Street; indeed, it is perfectly possible that the two families knew each other. Albert's father was a skilled joiner working for the famous local building firm Bowman and Sons. Mr Dunn was educated in Stamford and finished his schooling just around the corner from his home (on the Recreation Ground Road) at the St Michael's boys' school[1]. Stamford was a very different place in the early 1900s. Here are a few memories related to me by Mr Dunn from his school days:

- At four years old, he remembered his father leaving to fight in the First World War. His father was one of the lucky ones that returned afterwards.
- He remembered the fun all the boys of the town had in playing with a First World War tank that had been placed on the recreation grounds for exactly such a purpose; he recalls that the tank did get rather smelly inside.
- A good way to earn money as a teenager was to offer to look after local farmers' livestock when they stood in the streets of Stamford. Many livestock sales were held in Ironmonger Street, the High Street, etc., and the shops in the town would all have big wooden shutters to protect their glass fronts and doors from the animals. The youths would form a circle around the cattle, horses, or sheep to

[1] *Editor's note*: The name 'St Michael's boys' school' was a local given name. At the time of Mr Dunn's attendance, this school was named Stamford Boys' School. This was a different school to the 'Boys' School' of recent local parlance, which referred to Stamford School (based around St Paul's Street); this school, in turn, is now part of the co-educational Stamford Schools.

keep them together while the farmer would visit a local pub for refreshment (in Stamford, there was no shortage of public houses in the town centre). The boys would be rewarded upon the farmer's return – provided all of the animals were present and intact – with the extent of the youths' remuneration often dependent on how tipsy the farmer was.

When Albert left school he started work as an apprentice ironmonger at (yes, I am sure you've guessed it) Mr Tommy Duncomb's at 5–6 High Street. Mr Harrison was, by now, a top front counter shop hand, the year being 1924. The country was in a very deep recession; jobs were in short supply, and Albert was lucky to get this employment. By this time, however, T.S. Duncomb had grown to be a large employer in the town.

T.S. DUNCOMB, IRONMONGER

The shop premises at 5–6 High Street had continued to be improved. They had extended into Wellington Lane through to Red Lion Street, and special workshops had been built to include tin and copper smiths, blacksmiths, and mower repairs and sharpening. It was a grand ironmonger's at which to learn the trade, with so many different skills to gain. The variety of services and items on offer seems, today, quite remarkable. The large worktop which fronted onto the Broad Street end was for agricultural goods and 'hot water engineers' (we now call them 'plumbers'). They were specialists in installing heating systems, and did so in many large local houses, halls, and churches. At one time they sold ESSE cookers, which were capable of running large kitchens plus heating radiators. Notice in *Figure 5* the range of goods for sale (not to mention the interesting 'non explosive air gas plant' – I wonder who manufactured it?). Mr Dunn remarked that it was quite common for a customer to come into the

Figure 5†: An advert for T.S. Duncomb, ironmonger.

shop on, say, a Monday, order a complete set of saucepans or kettles to their own specifications, and then to call in the following weekend to collect them.

The premises at number 6 High Street had previously been the London and North Western Railway Parcel Receiving & Enquiry Office. This large space was now an open showroom for T.S. Duncomb, although the entrance to the shop remained at number 5 High Street (in 1934, however, Mr Duncomb would sell number 5 to Montague Burton, the tailor, and number 6 became the sole premises of the ironmonger's). During the Stamford Fair of St Simon and St Jude (an annual two-day fair of horses and sheep on the 9th of November and of cattle and 'beasts' on the 10th of November; by this time, it was held in the new cattle market at St Martin's), this large showroom would be set with large banqueting tables and chairs, and all of the farmers would be invited to dine there. Mr Dunn remembers those two days for all of the food, wine, and beer he served. He also recalled that, after their dinner, the farmers would take out their gold sovereigns and settle their outstanding bills with Duncomb's – a year of monies owed from all those customers settled on a single day.

Mr Dunn continued his apprenticeship with the best of training, working alongside the top front counter salesman, Mr Harrison. The competition between different firms in Stamford was considerable, with rival firms competing for both domestic and professional customers. Competitors for Duncomb's included Mr Grimes' shop in St Mary's Street, Baker's on St Mary's Hill, Chas Gray on Wharf Road, and Ellis & Everard's. In those days, the retail price index meant most goods carried the same prices (the first cut-price argument began with Woolworth's stores: while the quality of their goods was reputedly very much lower, nonetheless they began a new competitive element in the town). A shop known as the Penny Bazaar that was situated opposite Duncomb's, on the High Street, sold cheap enamel buckets on display in the street outside. According to Mr Dunn, the apprentices at Duncomb's would go up to the attic and would throw handfuls of lead shot out of the window at the buckets opposite in order to chip small holes in them. Whether Mr Duncomb knew of this practice we don't know, although given his shrewd behaviour it is easy to suspect that he did. Mr Dunn stated that the working day began at 6.30am, and would not end until Mr Duncomb drove into town in his large car (one of the few in Stamford at the time) and allowed them to close. He would only do this when there were no customers in sight on the High Street, and often the shop would not close until after 9pm.

OVERCOMING ADVERSITY

Mr Harrison and Mr Dunn had struck up a friendship while working together, being firm friends by the end of Mr Dunn's training (see *Figure 6*). Albert had learned his trade through the years of wealth and excess synonymous with the 'Roaring Twenties', but the United Kingdom was soon to find itself plunged into the Great Depression that followed the London and Wall Street stock exchange crashes of 1929 (caused by the overconfident stock market speculation the prosperity of the Roaring Twenties had encouraged). With the early 1930s economy looking bleak (by 1931, some three million people nationwide would be unemployed), Mr Duncomb decided not to continue Mr Dunn's employment beyond the completion of his apprenticeship. Already disappointed, Mr Dunn was further upset to hear that Mr Duncomb had arranged employment for him with another ironmonger in Bradford, Yorkshire (it was common for an employer not to want a former employee to work for a local competitor, for fear that advantageous secrets of their business would be revealed).

Albert Dunn had begun courting one Winifred Plowright, a local girl that worked as a seamstress in Stamford High Street. Not wanting to leave his life in Stamford, Mr Dunn began to think of a way out of his predicament. While talking to his friend Mr Harrison of his dilemma, Albert put forward the idea of opening his own ironmonger's shop, and was surprised when Mr Harrison commented that he thought it to be a good idea and that he would be willing to join him in his venture. They therefore set out to do just that.

When Mr Duncomb received notice of this from his two employees, he was immediately furious, and declared that he would do all in his power to prevent them from succeeding in their plan. He immediately informed all of his suppliers that if any of them dealt with this new firm, he himself would no

Figure 6: Albert Dunn, pictured here in the late 1920s/early 1930s, around the time that he completed his apprenticeship.

longer purchase from them. He also spoke to local estate agents and asked them not to assist Mr Dunn and Mr Harrison in procuring premises. In spite of Mr Duncomb's threats, the two new partners formed their new firm, Harrison & Dunn, and, if anything, were made more determined to succeed by the adversity they faced.

However, Mr Duncomb was as good as his word, and they were unable to find anywhere available for rent. Eventually, after talking to a Miss Lee of St Peter's Street, who had been left a number of properties by her father, they secured a small shop from her at 10 All Saints' Street. Now they could turn to the problem of preparing it for business, a problem that Albert's brother, Eddie, a local carpenter and joiner, contributed a great deal to solving by constructing shelves, show stands, and counters. The two new partners were now ready to stock the shop, but again found that Mr Duncomb had made good on his threats: no local wholesalers would supply them, not with the risk of losing the business of an established shop like Duncomb's.

With no stock, the newly procured and furnished Harrison & Dunn shop would be no good. Fortunately, the two partners had a plan to overcome their supply issue. Mr Harrison owned a motorbike and sidecar (similar to that shown in *Figure 7*) and so the two of them set off for Birmingham, the city that was home to the main wholesalers in ironmongery. The plan was to visit each one face to face in order to strike up a business relationship; but even here they found that Mr Duncomb's influence had spread, and all refused to trade with them.

A SAVIOUR IS FOUND

All, that is, except one. On visiting Thomas Plant wholesalers

Figure 7: A motorbike and sidecar similar to that owned by Mr Harrison (image reproduced by kind permission of F2 Motorcycles Ltd).

(with premises near the Bull Ring area), they found that the boss himself, Mr Thomas Plant, had taken offence at Mr Duncomb's threats. He therefore said that he would be happy to supply them. The condition was that they had to pay cash, so Albert, armed with a pocket full of money, did so, and soon they were biking back to Stamford with a sidecar full of saucepans, tools, and general ironmongery.

Once back in their shop, they set to work marking their stock and filling up the shop window display. They had both decided to have a policy of selling their stock at reasonable prices, and this policy soon paid off. The stock on display was sold out on the first day of trading, and next day Mr Dunn was back on the motorbike to Thomas Plant's, armed with the money that had been made. This became a pattern over the next weeks and months: Mr Dunn doing the buying in Birmingham while Mr Harrison did the selling in Stamford.

Upon seeing the quantity of goods the new shop was selling (and the number of miles Mr Dunn was covering on the motorbike), Thomas Plant allowed Harrison & Dunn, Stamford, to open a credit account, and stated that whatever stock they ordered would be sent to Stamford by train.

And so it was that arriving at Stamford Midland railway station[2] each week were many large wicker baskets filled with ironmongery, which were in turn transported each day to the Harrison & Dunn shop by Mr Sharpe, the carrier, with his horse and cart. 10 All Saints' Street had a small backyard where the goods would be unpacked, and the yard was always covered in the straw that was used to pack between the goods. This straw had to be constantly gathered, packed back into the empty baskets, and then the baskets had to have their lids fixed down and be returned to Birmingham.

[2] *Editor's note*: This Stamford Midland station is the same station as today's Stamford station, and at that time was properly called Stamford Town. It was one of two stations in Stamford in the 1930s, the second being the now-closed Stamford East station (the building for this second station still stands today on the corner of Water Street and Welland Mews).

CHAPTER 2

BECOMING ESTABLISHED

A VIBRANT MERCHANT TOWN

In those days, All Saints' Street was a very good place to trade: it had many more shops than it does today. Here is a brief 'snapshot' of the street around the time that Harrison & Dunn started trading:

The street had three public houses: The Mill Stone, The Wheat Sheaf, and the Albion Tavern. It also, of course, had the Melbourns' brewery, at the time in full swing producing all of its own beers. Then, at the top of the street, moving down one side: at number 2 was the butcher's, Cunnington's; at number 3 was Bassendines, the draper's (not a very large shop in those days); number 4 was a hairdresser's; number 5 was a Singer's sewing machines vendor; number 6, the Hit It Out outfitter's; at number 7 was Dodman's, a confectioner; at number 8, Smith & Son umbrella makers; number 9, Tilley, the missuses' fancy repository (not sure what that was); number 10 was, of course, the new Harrison & Dunn shop; in number 11, next door, lived the Sargents, the family of the world-famous conductor Sir Malcolm Sargent; 12 was a private house, Mr Taylor; number 13 was the callises[3]. Then, going across the road and back up towards town: Wade's fish and chip shop; Boyden's upholsterer's and picture framing; 17 was quite a large shop: a newsagent, tobacconist, and toy shop; 18 was Peasgood, a builder and undertaker; 19, Old Fellows Hall; then Mr Gilbert's, fruiterer; next was Red Lion Square, with a busy post office and a butcher's shop next to it. On the corner: in my youth, we knew it as Harvey's Corner; in those days, though, Hicks' confectioners ran a shop there.

1931 was not a good time to run a business: the Great Depression was still making itself known. Stamford, though, was in a good position to weather this financial crisis. In those days, we (Stamford) were known as an engineering town with a very good base of manufacturing, namely in the world-famous Blackstone & Co., which started in the town in 1837. Developing out of the invention and manufacture of agricultural implements – via steam engines – Blackstone's was one of the first British firms to start making oil engines. By the 1930s, its diesel engines were being sold all over the world, and they employed hundreds and hundreds of workers. Stamford also had Arthur Lyon's (later to become Newage's,

[3] *Editor's note*: The author is here referring to the St Peter's Callis almshouses.

then Cummins as they are known today); Martin's Cultivators and Markham's Traction, both manufacturers of farming implements (and which would later merge to form Martin-Markham's); the Williamson Cliff brickyard and lime quarry; and of course our own borough council (as opposed to a shared district or county council): all very large employers in those days. All these firms were spending their money in Stamford.

FINDING ITS FEET

Soon, the new Harrison & Dunn shop prospered. The manufacturer and wholesaler firms' travellers (representatives of the firms that would visit stores to sell or promote their products), noticing in the shop's windows the things that their own firms produced, soon began to favour Messrs Harrison and Dunn and to ignore Mr Duncomb. Mr Dunn, who was still the buyer at that time, took up their offers and was in no time able to buy at more favourable prices, therefore enabling him to reduce the shop's retail prices.

It is worth recording here some of the money-saving habits that the new shop had adopted. Any string and paper that was used to wrap goods when they arrived from the manufacturers was carefully unfolded, saved, and reused to wrap goods for customers when sold (no plastic bags in those days, of course). Old bicycle inner tubes were collected from Hawley's bike shop in St Mary's Street; these were cut up into narrow sections to make rubber bands, and these would hold things together, like wooden pegs (pegs in bundles, in half-dozens, etc.). The marking of goods was also done in a very inexpensive way: they would use a marking ink with a dip pen. If the goods had a shiny surface, a small area would be rubbed with something of a powder, such as Vim, so that the ink could take to the surface. Funnily enough, even after sixty years, my wife has a set of cake tins that still show the ink prices on the base: the ink has never washed off (see *Figure 8*). The amount of information carried by these markings was quite incredible. In code, the markings would tell you where the goods were bought from, what price had been paid for them, and then, of course, the retail price. The till system comprised of pot pudding basins underneath the counter: one pot would be for pennies; one for tuppence; another for thruppence; for sixpence; for pounds; and so on.

Harrison & Dunn's started to increase its staff by employing a local boy straight from school as an errand boy in the town, one Reg Chambers. With his trade bike, he began to deliver around the town (Reg worked all his life for us, as many staff continue to do to this day). This relieved Mr Harrison of some of his work, and he was now able to make more contact with all of his old customers who lived around

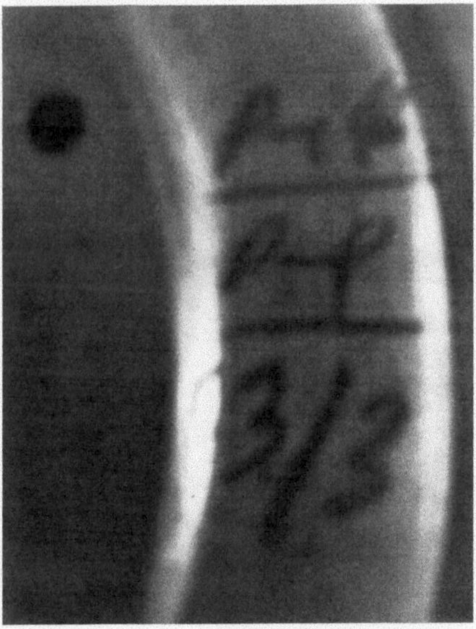

Figure 8: Cake tins still showing Harrison & Dunn price markings.

the villages. He would visit them with his motorbike and sidecar, taking orders and selling them goods. Soon, they bought their first van, a small Model T Ford at a cost of two pound ten shillings (see *Figure 9*). In those days there were no supermarkets, and very few people owned a car. Thus, those from the countryside rarely or never visited Stamford. They would have instead have found transport to visit nearby shops once or twice a month. This was when Mr Dunn began to formulate his idea for travelling shops; however, with the rise of Germany's Third Reich and the dark clouds of war gathering, he would have to shelve his ideas.

Figure 9: A picture from the 1930s of Albert Dunn and possibly Mr Harrison in front of what appears to be the Harrison & Dunn Ford Model T van. Pictured left to right are: Albert Dunn; one Arthur Boyden (his son James Boyden in front of him); somebody that I believe could be Mr Harrison; and Albert's brother, Eddie Dunn.

1934 was the year in which Mr Dunn married his long-term girlfriend, Winifred. He lived with his in-laws in Doughty Street. Mr Harrison had also got married and had moved into a new house in Queen's Walk. The shop in the '30s specialised in tools for all trades: joiners, bricklayers, and, of course, lots of engineering tools (see the advertisements in *Figure 10*). They also became large sellers of heating oil (as

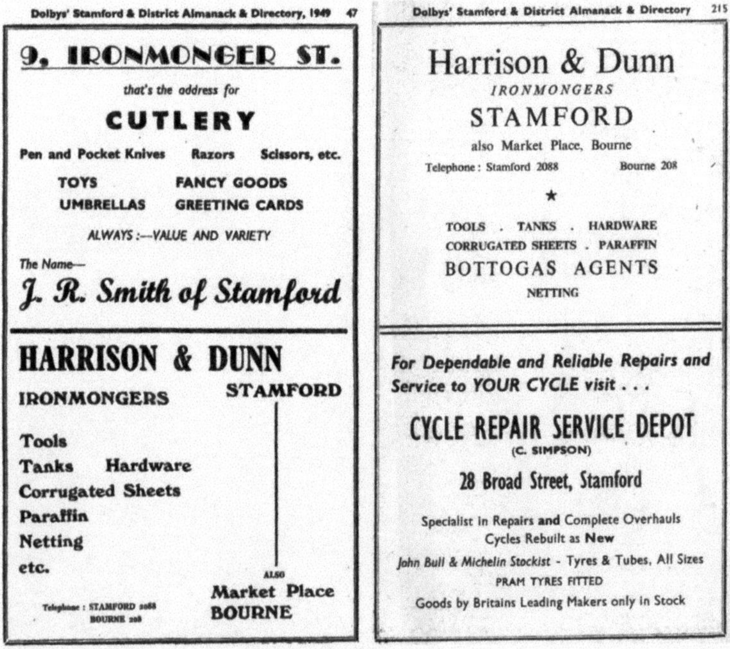

Figure 10†: Advertisements for Harrison & Dunn in Dolby's Stamford and District Almanack & Directory, 1949 (left) and pre-1950s (right).[4]

[4] Note the advert for dear old Mrs Smith's shop at number 9 Ironmonger Street. If you went into her so small shop and asked for, say, a birthday card, she would go off out the back of the shop, up the stairs, and return with two or three. She was so nice that she would go back and forth until you had one you were happy with.

we call it now, paraffin) and they also sold liquid gas in metal bottles. Mr and Mrs Dunn moved into a new semi-detached house in Empingham Road, his in-laws moving with them to a new house next door.

THE SECOND WORLD WAR

1939 saw the start of the Second World War. Given that the shop was considered a vital supplier of fuel, Mr Dunn, as owner, was considered too important to call up; Mr Harrison was considered too old. Reg, however, was granted no exemption, and was very soon called into the army. Mr Dunn joined the Civil Defence Service (which took up a lot of Mr Dunn's spare time even after the war, until 1946) and also worked in a munitions factory in Peterborough. 1940 saw the first increase to his family, with a daughter, Sheila, being born in May (I myself having come into the world that very year two months before her). With Mr Harrison spending most of his time serving in the shop, the war years passed: distressing news, however, had reached them that Reg had been captured by the Japanese in the Far East. In 1945, a son, Richard, was born to Albert and Winifred, completing the Dunn family.

The trading life of Stamford soon improved as things returned to normal after the war. Some larger shops started to enter the town – such as Woolworths store, International Stores, Maple, Home and Colonial, Eayrs, Parker, etc. – all sticking to their own trade of groceries. There were also now twelve butcher's shops in the town and five ironmonger's.

It was believed that Reg had not survived the Japanese forced labour camps, as nothing had been heard from or about him for many years. While at the factory in Peterborough, Mr Dunn worked alongside and befriended a Jim Dickson, and so offered him the now vacant position at the shop. Then

– good news! – they were informed that Reg was in fact okay, and returned back to Stamford and, of course, his job. This gave Harrison & Dunn a problem as they would now have a staff of four: too many for their small shop. Mr Dunn solved the matter by leasing a shop in Bourne (this was in 1946), which Mr Dickson began to run. This increased the buying power of Harrison & Dunn, as all goods sold in Bourne were supplied from Stamford, an arrangement still in place today.

THE TRAVELLING SHOPS

Mr Dunn's idea of a travelling shop became a reality with the purchase of their first lorry (see *Figure 11*). The lorry was a 1931 model Bedford, with the back taken off and a large tank installed for the carrying and dispensing of paraffin. The lorry proved to be so successful that soon they were planning their much larger, carefully designed, specialised Harrison & Dunn lorry (see *Figures 12–17*). Two large paraffin tanks were directly fixed onto a Bedford lorry chassis (purchased from a local firm, Forsyth & Ferrier); then, on top of that, was a large wooden back with rolling shutters either side, custom-made by a Leicester firm called Syston's (who are still in business today) (see *Figures 15–16*). Soon, there were two mobile shops, identical in design, and covering a large area of the countryside.

Reg became a well-known driver after his return from the war, and he made a working partnership for life in Arthur Thrift. Here I include the memories of Mr Bluff, who was another of the van drivers in the 1950s:

> When I joined Harrison & Dunn in 1958, they had two mobile shops, both Bedfords based on 3-ton chassis.

Figure 11: Harrison & Dunn's first travelling shop, a 1931 Bedford van, taken outside Reg Chambers' house on Lincoln Road, Stamford.

Figure 12: One of Harrison & Dunn's travelling shops, an adapted Bedford lorry.

Figure 13: One of Harrison & Dunn's travelling shops, an adapted Bedford lorry.

Figure 14: One of Harrison & Dunn's travelling shops, an adapted Bedford lorry.

Figure 15: Side view of one of Harrison & Dunn's travelling shops, clearly showing the shutters.

Figure 16: Side view of one of Harrison & Dunn's travelling shops with shutters open, revealing how goods would be displayed.

Figure 17: A rare colour photograph of one of the later Harrison & Dunn travelling shops.

Down the centre, resting on the chassis, were two oblong galvanised tanks, each holding about 150 gallons of paraffin. These were filled and emptied at the rear.

Access to the shop was via three roller shutter doors on either side, allowing customers to view the goods carried. There was also a roof rack, reached by footholds up the rear of the van.

A wide range of cleaning materials was carried, plus soap, soap powders, disinfectants, etc., plus a range of tinned fruit and vegetables.

Hardware items carried included: tools, garden tools, rugs, mats, cooking utensils, crockery, ovenware, paraffin heaters and spares, paint, paint brushes, and other DIY equipment. On the roof rack would be rolls of wire netting, rolls of roofing felt, a wheelbarrow, two types of dustbin, a dolly tub, and sometimes bottled liquid gas (when ordered).

No perishable food was carried, except for a few weeks prior to Christmas when we had fancy tins of Peek Freans biscuits. There was an occasion when I was in the All Saints' Stamford shop a few days after the salesman had taken the orders for the biscuits. A large van stopped outside and the driver came into the shop, looking rather puzzled. He had a look around, then turned to leave, so I asked him if I could help.

'No,' he said. 'I must have been given the wrong address. I have forty cartons of tinned biscuits; obviously you don't want them here.'

I assured him he was at the right address.

The shops covered quite a large area between them. Both were out for five days each week, working on a fortnightly basis.

Most villages in Rutland were visited. Some of the trips I can recall: Tallington, West Deeping, Maxey, Etton, and Helpston; Seaton, Lyddington, Gretton, and Harringworth; Careby, Little Bytham, and Castle Bytham; Bulwick, Deene, Deenethorpe, and Weldon; Bisbrooke, Caldecott, and Great Easton; Thornhaugh, Wansford, Yarwell, and Nassington.

On Saturdays, Mr A. Dunn himself would take to the road, calling at Dyke, Dowsby, Dunsby, and Rippingale. The following week it would be Morton, Kirkby Underwood, Aslackby, Pointon, and Billingborough.

The vans' staff would be acquainted with so many people living in the surrounding villages, taking their orders one visit for delivery the next. The shop also ran a book scheme, whereby customers would receive their goods and pay so much a week over subsequent weeks to pay for them. Many people still fondly remember to me the regular visits of the vans as part of their childhood: an exciting and much-loved event in village life that would set local dogs a-barking. As well as these warm memories of the mobile shops themselves, many old tradesmen tell me how they still own the tools purchased from Harrison & Dunn (who would always give tradesmen a 10% discount) – saws, chisels, etc. – that started their working lives. Mr Dunn took very seriously the fact that the shop was a supplier of fuel, and many were the days when he insisted the vans travelled when it was not safe to – through snow and ice – in order to ensure the delivery of paraffin.

Mr Dunn would often take the smaller van out himself to supplement the deliveries of oil. His daughter, Sheila, recalled to me that she always pestered him to bring her back a kitten from his village round. As he never did, she once insisted that he take her with him so she could find one herself. In the end, when she was aged ten, he agreed; however, Sheila found that she could not bear the smell of paraffin, and he had to stop to let her out of the van as she felt sick. 'Never again,' he said – and Sheila still had no kitten.

THE 1950s: THE BUSINESS EXPANDS

Harrison & Dunn now owned two mobile shops (with a total of four drivers), had employed a greater number of staff in the Stamford shop, and had increased the staff in the Bourne shop to two (see advert for the shops in *Figure 18*). Sheila worked in the shop from a very young age – whilst still at school – with

Figure 18†: An advert for Harrison & Dunn, 1955.

Figure 19: A tea set stacked as on the Harrison & Dunn vans (a modern demonstration by my wife, Sheila).

no wages. When she left school in 1956, she joined the firm full-time. She recalls the list of all the van orders, according to which she would select the appropriate goods and prepare them for loading onto the vans on the correct days. A typical list would consist of blancmanges and jellies, tins of peas, tinned fruit, kitchen utensils, dustbins, wire netting, washing powders, ironmongery, and tea sets. The tea sets would be stacked up in a row just as on this shelf (see *Figure 19*). This goes to show what a good steady driver was needed for the mobile shops, as we never heard of any breakages.

My interest in ironmongery began in 1956 – or, shall I say, my interest in an ironmonger's daughter – when I started going out with Sheila. I had started work as a carpenter and joiner apprentice (indented to the Burghley Estate building depot) and – what with Sheila working there – started buying all my ironmongery at Harrison & Dunn; I was after much more than the discount.

The two partners looked at expanding the shop's size, and to that end purchased next door, number 11 All Saints' Street (the previous home of Sir Malcolm Sargent's family). Soon, Bowman's (the builders) joined through next door: removing internal walls, and installing two good-sized plate glass windows and a small centre six-sided window. The 'new showroom' (the name given to the new floors) was really for Sheila to deal with, and was her domain. She recalls that not many customers would go upstairs, but that she took great pleasure in displaying pots, kitchen utensils, units, door mats, and new lines in kitchen cabinets from Fleetwood (which were made near Blackpool). The small window in the new showroom became a great draw for the locals, as Sheila would fill it daily with special offers and bargain goods.

The shop was still selling thousands of gallons of paraffin a week, with regular van rounds continuing in the towns and villages. The vans were now garaged in what used to be the Esso petrol depot in Hallidays Yard, Radcliffe Road. This gave Harrison & Dunn a very large capacity for the storage of Esso Blue paraffin, storing it in old petrol tanks which were sunk into the ground. The mobile shops, which would be parked there overnight, would have their tanks filled early in the morning by means of a hand pump system, way before 6.30am. When the tanks were full, the vans would then go down to the back of the shop for loading up with the stock for each day. In this way, by about 7.00 to 7.30am they were ready to set off (the shop itself would open from 7.30am, a tradition still kept today). Not only was loose paraffin sold from the vans and the shop: loose vinegar (which was really unbrewed condiment) and also creosote could be purchased in your own cans. The drivers were set as fixed teams: one, Reg Chambers and Archie Thrift worked together. Jack Toon was also a long-time driver for Harrison & Dunn, and many others who came and then moved on.

CHAPTER 3

TAKING OWNERSHIP

ALBERT MAKES ACQUISITIONS

Mr Dunn had realised that Mr Harrison would retire much earlier than himself, and so had built up the cash reserves of the firm in readiness to pay him out. This happened in 1960, and Mr Harrison duly took all of his money out of the firm (he had no children to carry on his share of the business). He left the town, and had a short retirement in Skegness.

The highlight of Mr Dunn's business career also happened in this year, when he discovered that his old firm where he had learned his apprenticeship, Duncomb & Co., was in a state of financial difficulty. Imagine his delight, after all that Tommy Duncomb had done to prevent him from succeeding. Mr Dunn was able to buy the business and prevent it from going into receivership. As he had just paid out his partner, the firm had to take out a loan to cover the cost, particularly as very shortly after this Mr Dunn also bought Duncomb's premises on the High Street. See *Figure 20* for an advert for Harrison & Dunn alongside Duncomb & Co.

Sheila remembers her father sending her up to the High Street shop to sort it out with new stock. She was shocked by the lack of saleable stock she found there, and the lack of good displays in the shop. It was still run like a Victorian shop, with bolts and fastenings still sold wrapped in small parcels of brown paper tied up with string (not in boxes as they are today, and indeed as in most establishments then). Mr Dunn retained the existing staff; however, Sheila found them to be resistant to her attempts to bring in changes of stock. This was perhaps hardly surprising given how long the staff had been associated with Duncomb's: two of the staff, Jack and Claude Wharton, were previous owners of the shop, and their father, Mr Wharton, had been a partner to Tommy Duncomb and had taken over when Mr Duncomb died in 1949.

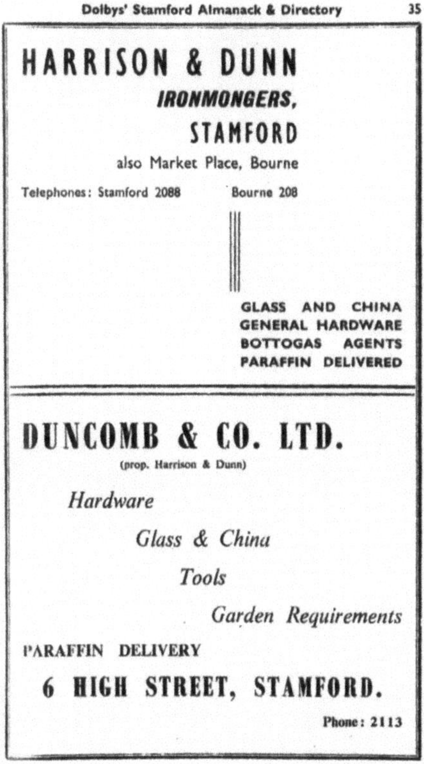

Figure 20†: An advert for Harrison & Dunn and Duncomb & Co. Ltd side by side, 1965.

ALBERT CHALLENGES ME

1961 saw Harrison & Dunn become a truly family affair, with Mr Dunn's son, Richard, going to work at the shop straight from leaving school. Around this time I had completed my apprenticeship, and moved onto general building and civil engineering with Stamford Construction. I still visited Harrison & Dunn to buy much of the goods for my building needs. My best acquisition from the shop, however, was in that year of 1961, when I married Sheila and moved into a bungalow in Radcliffe Close, which I am happy to say has given us both sixty-three years, so far, of happiness. We had three children in the Swinging Sixties: Judith, Andrew, and Karen.

My career in the building and civil engineering trade was to last until 1967, when, to save time instead of going to Harrison & Dunn, I visited Duncomb's for a padlock I required, it being en route to Harrison & Dunn on the High Street (I was able to park outside, the traffic then running in both directions). I was shocked to see the state of the shop and by the attitude of the staff: not at all helpful, and, in fact, they had not got the padlock that I wanted. I was far from pleased, and told them as much, my day delayed as I now still had to continue on to Harrison & Dunn after all. When collecting the padlock at Harrison & Dunn, I was therefore in a bit of a mood, and so was telling the assistant – I can't remember who it was that was serving me – what a disgrace the shop on the High Street was and that something should be done about it. I must have been talking quite loudly because Mr Dunn, having heard me, came out of the office and said:

'Well, what would you do about it?'

I said, 'I don't know, but something needs to be done.'

'Well,' he said, 'you come up with a plan and we'll look at it.'

Over the next few weeks, I familiarised myself with the layout of Duncomb's, looking at the inside of the shop displays and pestering the staff with quite a few visits. When I was ready, and after discussing it with my wife, Sheila, my plans to bring the High Street shop into the 1960s were laid out before my father-in-law. They were ambitious, with considerable building alterations (which, if adopted, would have enlarged the shop floor some ten times) and a completely new internal layout, making the shop a modern walk-around DIY store. To my surprise, Mr Dunn thought the idea good, but said could I 'price out the cost of the construction, please'. I estimated the cost to carry out the building alterations and realised that the cost was very considerable.

It was then that an idea came to me. By then, working in the building and civil engineering industry had become, to me, very stressful. Not in the construction sense, but in the amount of corruption in the industry. I had been in charge of contracts for many millions of pounds, but some officials involved who should have been looking after the public money – making sure it was being spent correctly – were more interested in accepting bribes (and similar such arrangements) and I was not happy being a part of this. I was struck by the thought of taking on the job of personally altering Duncomb's premises. My wife was not sure that I should take on such a task when I was, after all, doing so well in my chosen profession. Nevertheless, I presented a plan to carry out the building work myself.

Mr Dunn was delighted, and we discussed how the proposal might work. I estimated the work would take at least one year, so we came up with an agreement that Harrison & Dunn would pay me a weekly wage and pay all the bills for the building materials and plant. The plans for building regulations and planning permission I carried out myself, and once the Stamford Borough Council had granted these, I gave notice to my employer.

I ROLL UP MY SLEEVES

The first job (which was very daunting to begin with) was to empty the storerooms and workshops at the back of the Duncomb's shop. It was obvious to me why Duncomb's had gone down and down, because the stock that had never been sold – for whatever reason – was there to be seen. The sheer amount of this old stock shocked me, an amount that did not seem to reduce even after many months of dirty work. I would start very early in the morning, well before the High Street shops would open, and put out lots of old stock in the side lane, Wellington Lane, which runs down the side of 6 High Street, Stamford; I took considerable amounts of cash selling it off.

The things that I was trying to clear from the back rooms were amazing, some of them going right back to Victorian days. For example, old cast iron ranges, which had cast iron cooking centres, a water tank one side, and a cooker the other. There were old delivery handcarts, old plumbing fittings. I started to ask local antique dealers to visit the back rooms and see what they might want; I sold a lot of old stock to them. I also started to tackle the old lead and brass plumbing fittings and take them to the scrap merchants Lee & Company. After about four months, the storerooms were nearly empty. I was getting frustrated, anxious to start the building work in order to keep to my estimate of one year to completion.

At last, the last of the stock was clear.

I started the construction work by inserting RSJs – steel beams – into the three walls to be removed. I can well remember my wife, Sheila, visiting me on the job with our son when he would only be about two years old. Andrew was soon copying me, helping his dad: while I was knocking down the large stone walls and taking the stone away in my barrow, so he would pick up small pieces of stone and carry them in his walker. During the building work, I only asked for help when there were heavy items to lift. I enjoyed very much carrying on the brickwork, connecting the drain work, the plumbing, the carpentry and the joinery work (I did have some help with painting the walls and ceilings). The only other tradesmen I used were a plasterer for ceilings and one for electrical work, which was carried out by John Banks, who worked for Feetham electrical, High Street.

The most loved sounds during my year of work came from my small transistor radio, with the new Beatles number ones 'Lady Madonna' and 'Hey Jude' playing, along with their thirteen other number ones previous to these. There were also a few female voices to help me along my way, such as Marianne Faithfull and Sandie Shaw.

During this year, I wanted to get a feel for the ironmonger's trade, so I worked in the front shop as a sales person every Saturday. This was so that I could plan the best layout for the different goods in the new shop.

I had kept to my deadline of one year to complete the building work. In the end, setting out the different departments was by far the most exciting part of the project, and I so wanted to see if my ideas worked that I asked Mr Dunn if I could stay and run the shop, to see how my designs played out. Mr Dunn was not only agreeable but suggested that I become a director of Duncomb & Co., and a partner in Harrison & Dunn. A partnership agreement was entered into which included Mr and Mrs Dunn, Richard Dunn, and myself, Michael Lee.

THE NEW DUNCOMB'S

It was quite a task to stock the new shop with not only all the different goods that Harrison & Dunn sold but also with many more lines which I introduced, including fitted kitchens and bathrooms (supplied and fitted), timber doors, plumbing, Conti board and similar building supplies, and lots of other DIY goods. Both shops in Stamford relied mainly on two lines: in the winter, it was paraffin heaters and oil; and in the summer, lawnmowers and garden requests.

The staff that I had inherited from Duncomb's: one Wharton brother, Jack, fitted in with the new way of trading, mainly carrying out the office work; the other brother, Claude, who had very fixed ideas, left our employ, but not before he had passed on to me his considerable skills in locksmithing and window displays, for which I was extremely grateful (Claude had been one of the young Spitfire pilots in the Battle of Britain, 1940); two ladies, Mrs Bluff and Mrs Snowden, continued to work for us. I had to increase the staff, however, due it being a much larger shop. I started two other workers, one part-time and the other full. The full-time employee was Christine Gregory (now Burrows), a girl more or less straight from school. She was a keen and hard worker, still with Harrison & Dunn today after fifty years. Her sister, Helen, joined Harrison & Dunn a little time later, and also continues to work there.

We did not change the name of the High Street shop, and it continued as Duncomb & Co. Ltd. I was very pleased with the way the new shop was working. The bulk of the stock for the shop was marked and supplied from the Harrison & Dunn store and transported to us each morning (*early* in the morning, by yours truly). The High Street was in those days an open road for vehicles. By 1970, the two shops were both successful. With the shop in the High Street specialising in fitted kitchens and bathrooms, timber, and DIY, and Harrison & Dunn specialising in tools and domestic goods, the two shops complemented the town.

CHAPTER 4

THE 1970s

THE CHANGING HIGH STREET

So, my personal involvement in the running of Harrison & Dunn and of Duncomb & Co. – as well as a turn as the President of the Chamber of Trade – started in 1968 onwards. The 1970s saw such great changes both locally and nationally, all of which affected retail in Stamford in general and Harrison & Dunn in one way or another.

I start by recording the start of the big change to retailing in the country, which was the onslaught of large out-of-town supermarkets (which came here as started in the USA). This firstly killed off all the specialist grocers in our high streets. For interest, I here reprint a copy of *Dolby's Stamford Almanack & Directory* for the High Street (see *Figures 21–23*): this clearly shows that, even in 1964, you could still buy anything you needed in our High Street – specialist shops in most trades. Sadly, by the early 1970s, all the grocers had closed. These included: number 8 High Street, Eayrs; number 9, the Maypole dairy; number 14, the International Stores; number 41 was the Co-op; 55, Mason's; and number 58, Home and Colonial.

234 STAMFORD DIRECTORY

Highlands Way continued
19 Kemp, P. E., B.Sc.
19aJones, R.
21 Regis, T.
23 Dolby, N. V.
25 Thorpe, A. G.
27 Groom, G. W.
29 Barlow, A. G., " Kenbar "
31 Gladstone, P.
33 Bagshaw, R. H.
35 Jackman, A.
37 Hardy, J. T.
39 Liston, M. J.
41 Long, R.
43 Hare, S. F.
45 Baxter, J. S.
47 Williams, C.
49 Towers, T. A.
51 Cardell, K. M., " Keanon "
53 Yuledon, K.
2 Kirk, R. C.
2aKettle, C.
4 Holmes, M. E.
6 Hayre, D. E.
8 Coates, O. M.
10 Revens, W. M.
12 Bodgers, A.
14 Hibbins, R. W.
16 Brown, B. S.
18 Bells, A.
20 Clark, A. J.
22 Forman, K. D.
24 Wilmott, R., " Glencruitten"
26 Knight, J.
28 Campell, O.
30 Stewart, G. C.
32 Dennis, D. A.
34 Engels, C. E.
36 Butcher, C.
38 Banks, P.
40 Clark, W.
42 Hetherington, R.
44 Hunter, W. J.
46 Harris, J. A.
48 Harvey, H. G.
50 Giddings, R.
52 Cotterill, A.
54 Ward, H. G. A.
56 Hill, G. W.
58 Divers, K. C.

HIGH STREET
1 Midland Bank Ltd.,
Slater, W., manager

High Street continued
3 Rodgers & Son, jewellers' watchmakers
3aCoombes, boot and shoe repairers
3bHolland, S. M.
4 Chapman & Son, drapers
Harrison, W. A., proprietor
5 Montague Burton Ltd., tailors
Billiard Hall—Lilley, W. A.
6 Duncomb & Co., Ltd., furnishing ironmongers
Wellington Lane
Davis, Miss K. B.
Hayre, F., Sunday newspapers
Catering Services (Midlands) Ltd.
7 Davis, A. C., jeweller, watchmaker
8 Eayrs, T. & J., grocers
9 Maypole Dairy Co.
10 Parrish & Sons, drapers and milliners, Gothic House
11 Meesons, confectionery
12 Cundy Wallpaper Co., Ltd.
Silver Lane
Hassan, A. B.
Cundy, T. E. & Son, Ltd.
W. H. Sparham (manager)
13 Smith, Jas. & Son, dyers and cleaners
Prudential Assurance Co., Ltd.
Superintendent, G. W. Gray
13aWoodcocks, home-made cakes
14 International Stores
McCully, J. J., manager
15 Smith, W. H. & Sons, stationers, James, L., manager
16 "Essiphit" Footwear,
Barnett, Miss B. A.
16aNiven, Mrs. A.
Lantern Restaurant & Cafe
Smith, Mrs.
17 Mac Fisheries
manager : Jones, R. F.
18 Sketchley Dye Works
Ward, Mrs. D., mageress
19 Taylor's Cash Chemists, London, Daccus, Mr., M.P.S., manager
20 Williams, W. A., greengrocer
21 Westmorelands (T.V. House)

Dolbys' Stamford Almanack & Directory 235

Tel. 2013
The
White Heather
Restaurant
Open from 9 a.m. to 6 p.m. (including Sundays)
MORNING COFFEES - LUNCHEONS - TEAS
FULLY LICENSED
PRIVATE PARTIES CATERED FOR
ALL SAINTS' PLACE - STAMFORD

PAULEY'S
FOR FRUIT AND VEGETABLES
Canteens Supplied Daily
Stamford Friday and Saturday Markets Attended
46 ST. PAUL'S STREET, STAMFORD
Telephone

Figure 21†: Stamford Directory, *Dolby's Stamford Almanack & Directory*, 1964, pages 234–235.

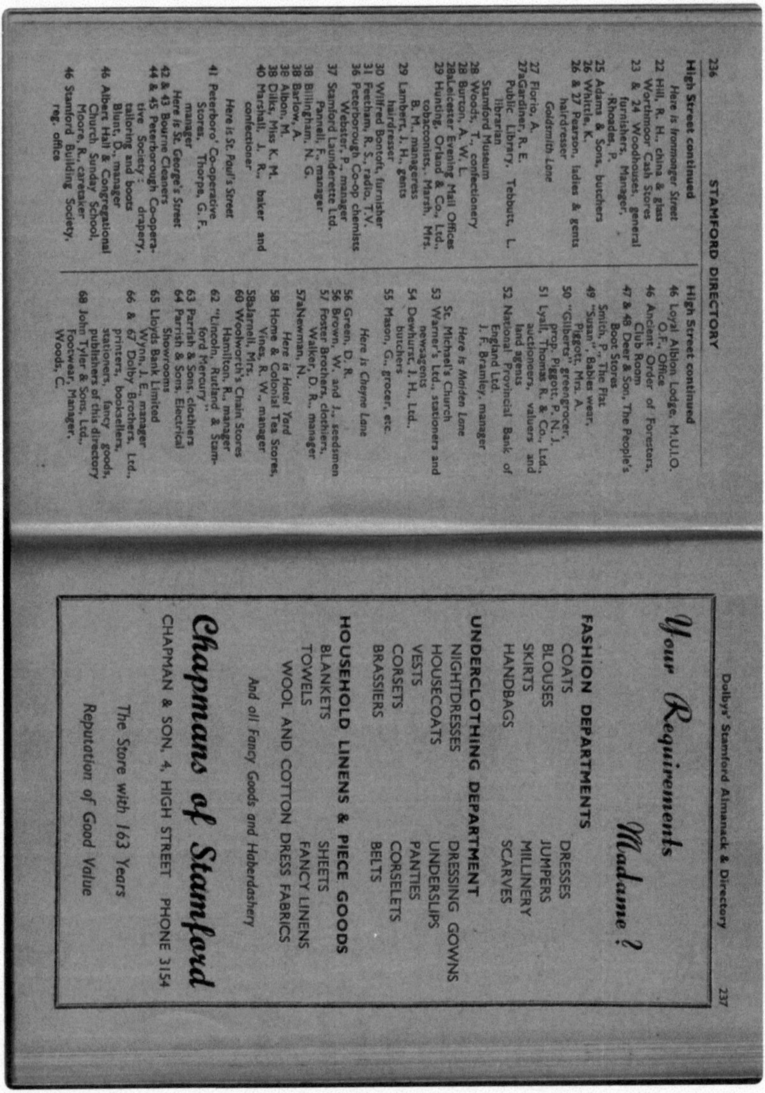
236 STAMFORD DIRECTORY

High Street continued

Here is Ironmonger Street

22 Hill, R. H., china & glass
Worthmoor Cash Stores
23 & 24 Woodhouses, general furnishers, Manager, Rhoades, P.
25 Adams & Sons, butchers
26 Whittle, K.
26 & 27 Pearson, ladies & gents hairdresser

Goldsmith Lane

27 Florio, A.
27aGardiner, R. E.
Public Library, Tebbutt, L. librarian
Stamford Museum
28 Woods, T., confectionery
28 Burton, A. W. L.
28aLeicester Evening Mail Offices
29 Hunting, Orland & Co., Ltd., tobacconists, Marsh, Mrs. B. M., manageress
29 Lambert, J. H., gents hairdresser
30 Wilfred Bontoft, furnisher
31 Feetham, R. S., radio, T.V.
36 Peterborough Co-op chemists Webster, P., manager
37 Stamford Launderette Ltd. Pannell, F., manager
38 Billingham, N. G.
38 Barlow, A.
38 Albon, M.
38 Dilks, Miss K. M.
40 Marshall, J. R., baker and confectioner

Here is St. Paul's Street

41 Peterboro' Co-operative Stores, Thorpe, G. F. manager

Here is St. George's Street

42 & 43 Bourne Cleaners
44 & 45 Peterborough Co-operative Society: drapery, tailoring and boots
Blunt, D., manager
46 Albert Hall & Congregational Church Sunday School, Moore, R., caretaker
46 Stamford Building Society, reg. office

High Street continued

46 Loyal Albion Lodge, M.U.I.O. O.F., Office
46 Ancient Order of Foresters, Club Room
47 & 48 Deer & Son, The People's Boot Stores
Smith, P., The Flat
49 "Susan", Babies wear, Piggott, Mrs. A.
50 "Gilberts" greengrocer, prop. Piggott, P. N. J.
51 Lyall, Thomas R. & Co., Ltd., auctioneers, valuers and land agents
52 National Provincial Bank of England Ltd.
J. F. Bramley, manager

Here is Maiden Lane

St. Michael's Church
53 Warner's Ltd., stationers and newsagents
54 Dewhurst, J. H., Ltd., butchers
55 Mason, G., grocer, etc.

Here is Cheyne Lane

56 Green, D. R.
56 Brown, W. and J., seedsmen
57 Foster Brothers, clothiers, Walker, D. R., manager
57aNewman, N.

Here is Hotel Yard

58 Home & Colonial Tea Stores, Vines, R. W., manager
58aJarnell, Mrs.
60 Woolworth's Chain Stores Hamilton, R., manager
62 "Lincoln, Rutland & Stamford Mercury"
63 Parrish & Sons, clothiers
64 Parrish & Sons, Electrical Showrooms
65 Lloyds Bank Limited Wynn, J. E., manager
66 & 67 Dolby Brothers, Ltd., printers, booksellers, stationers, fancy goods, publishers of this directory
68 John Tyler & Sons, Ltd., Footwear, Manager, Woods, C.

Dolbys' Stamford Almanack & Directory 237

Your Requirements Madame?

FASHION DEPARTMENTS

COATS DRESSES
BLOUSES JUMPERS
SKIRTS MILLINERY
HANDBAGS SCARVES

UNDERCLOTHING DEPARTMENT

NIGHTDRESSES DRESSING GOWNS
HOUSECOATS UNDERSLIPS
VESTS PANTIES
CORSETS CORSELETS
BRASSIERS BELTS

HOUSEHOLD LINENS & PIECE GOODS

BLANKETS SHEETS
TOWELS FANCY LINENS
WOOL AND COTTON DRESS FABRICS

And all Fancy Goods and Haberdashery

Chapmans of Stamford

CHAPMAN & SON, 4, HIGH STREET PHONE 3154

The Store with 163 Years Reputation of Good Value

Figure 22†: Stamford Directory, *Dolby's Stamford Almanack & Directory*, 1964, pages 236–237.

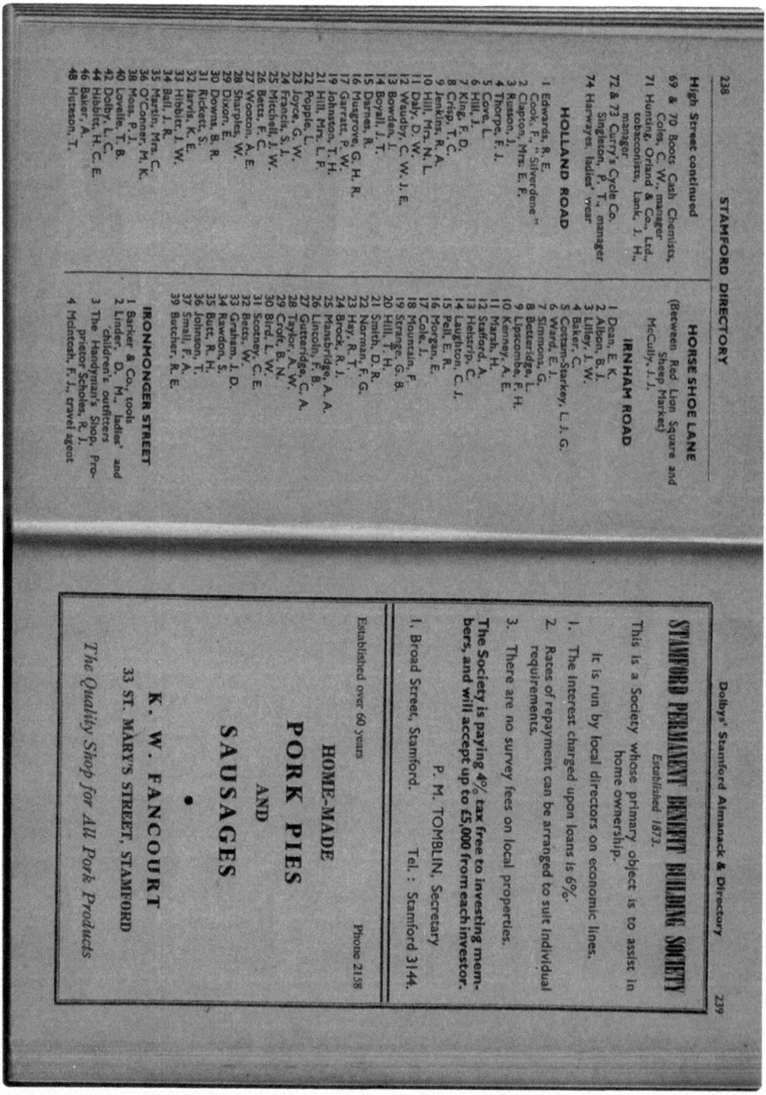

High Street continued

69 & 70 Boots Cash Chemists, Coles, C. W., manager
71 Hunting, Orland & Co., Ltd., tobacconists, Lank, J. H., manager
72 & 73 Curry's Cycle Co. Singleton, P. T., manager
74 Harwayes, ladies' wear

HOLLAND ROAD

1 Edwards, R. E.
Cook, F., " Silverdene "
2 Clapton, Mrs. E. F.
3 Russon, J.
4 Thorpe, F. J.
5 Cove, L.
6 Hill, J.
7 King, F. D.
8 Crisp, T. C.
9 Jenkins, R. A.
10 Hill, Mrs. N. L.
11 Daly, D. W.
12 Waudby, C. W. J. E.
13 Bowden, J.
14 Boyall, J. T.
15 Darnes, R.
16 Musgrove, G. H. R.
17 Garratt, P. W.
19 Johnston, T. H.
21 Hill, Mrs. L. F.
22 Popple, L.
23 Joyce, G. W.
24 Francis, S. J.
25 Mitchell, J. W.
26 Betts, F. C.
27 Wooton, A. E.
28 Sharples, W.
29 Dixon, E.
30 Downs, B. R.
31 Rickett, S.
32 Jarvis, K. E.
33 Hibbitt, J. W.
34 Ball, J. R.
35 Martin, Mrs. C.
36 O'Conner, M. K.
38 Moss, P. J.
40 Lovelle, T. B.
42 Dolby, L. C.
44 Hibbitt, H. C. E.
46 Baker, A.
48 Huteson, T.

HORSE SHOE LANE

(Between Red Lion Square and Sheep Market)
McCully, J. J.

IRNHAM ROAD

1 Dean, E. K.
2 Albon, B. J.
3 Lilley, J. W.
4 Baker, C.
5 Cottam-Starkey, L. J. G.
6 Ward, E. J.
7 Simmons, G.
8 Betteridge, L.
9 Lipscombe, F. H.
10 Kenney, A. E.
11 Marsh, H.
12 Stafford, A.
13 Helstrip, C.
14 Laughton, C. J.
15 Pell, E. R.
16 Morgan, E.
17 Cole, J.
18 Mountain, F.
19 Strange, G. B.
20 Hill, T. H.
21 Smith, D. R.
22 Norman, F. G.
23 Hay, R. T.
24 Brock, R. J.
25 Mansbridge, A. A.
26 Lincoln, F. B.
27 Gutteridge, C. A.
28 Taylor, A. W.
29 Croft, B. N.
30 Bird, L. W.
31 Scotney, C. E.
32 Betts, W.
33 Graham, J. D.
34 Rawdon, S.
35 Butt, R. H.
36 Johnson, T.
37 Small, F. A.
39 Butcher, R. E.

IRONMONGER STREET

1 Barker & Co., tools
2 Linder, D. M., ladies' and children's outfitters
3 The Handyman's Shop, Proprietor Scholes, R. J.
4 McIntosh, F. J., travel agent

Figure 23†: Stamford Directory, *Dolby's Stamford Almanack & Directory*, 1964, pages 234–235.

In Stamford, the first cut-price supermarket was opened by a local business family named Regis. It was called Sally Morland's, and it was situated in Green Lane. The cut-price DIY supermarkets out-of-town then started with shops in Stamford such as Focus. This started closing individual ironmonger's shops, whereas Harrison & Dunn and Duncomb's decided to continue our own policy of reasonable prices alongside personal service: a 'good morning'; a 'good afternoon, madam or sir'; an 'are you being served?'; or a 'can we help you?'. This – in my personal opinion – worked, and I'm happy to say that this principle is still the policy of Harrison & Dunn to the present day.

It is interesting to recall that around this time a general wholesale firm in Leicester that Mr Dunn had been dealing with for many years decided to open a local retail shop (in Leicester) called Wilkinson. When Mr Dunn discovered this, he was furious, and said that it was not fair (for it gave them two bites of the cherry, being both a wholesaler and a retailer). He vowed that Harrison & Dunn would never buy anything else from this particular firm, feeling sure that this would stop the firm from expanding. My wife later often passed comment, speaking to her dad in heaven, 'Well, I don't think that you won that one, Dad,' as we passed Wilkinson's massive Midlands supply depot, with hundreds of lorries waiting to supply hundreds of shops throughout the country.

So, with Harrison & Dunn's – complete with its shops in Stamford and Bourne and its two travelling shops – and Duncomb's – the modern, walk-around DIY store in the High Street – Harrison & Dunn continued trading. In the present day, we find that the cut-price DIY shops have actually raised their prices, as they had considered the individual traders killed off, and so today's Harrison & Dunn general goods are much cheaper than you find in these large shops.

In 1967, Stamford was listed as the first town of historical interest (the first conservation area in the UK), with many of the buildings being listed for preservation. 1971 saw national decimalisation day, when our country had to sadly say goodbye to the old currency of pounds, shillings, and pence. This involved quite a bit of work for retailers, with the Chamber of Trade arranging training for the staff of shops in order to be ready for the change to the new currency. It also involved lots of new decimalisation tills. Duncomb's bought a new decimalised till, and (much to the amusement of many of my staff) I additionally converted one of my old push-button tills by sticking new price labels on the buttons and the pop up signs (one shilling, for example, became five pence); however, this innovation didn't last very long, as the stickers soon came off or became illegible.

Things were different at the Harrison & Dunn shop, where Mr Dunn had long avoided using an expensive till even prior to decimalisation. He had persisted in using pudding basins below the counter for storing coins, and when the national till register man tried to sell a new till to Mr Dunn at Harrison & Dunn he replied, 'Oh no, it's okay, we will just add a few more pudding basins under the counter.' In reality, however, they had, by decimalisation, acquired an old wooden pull-out till, with a bell on top and a round paper roll upon which each sale would be recorded.

In 1971, Harrison & Dunn purchased next door, number 9 All Saints' Street, and I was once again busy with my building skills, knocking through to make Harrison & Dunn a larger shop and constructing a flat on the first floor. One day, whilst I was busy measuring up, I well remember my youngest daughter, Karen (who was aged about three at the time), falling from the top of the stairs at number 9 – bouncing down the stairs – and landing at the bottom with a great big smile on her face; she was a real tomboy, was my Karen.

Sheila and I had a very good time at all the social events in the town (see *Figure 24*). In those days, there were many grand balls held in Stamford, which were mostly held in the ballroom at the Assembly Rooms (which is now the Arts Centre) or on the sprung dance floor at Blackstones Social Club. There were farmers' balls, Licensed Victuallers' balls, Prize Stock Show, Chamber of Trade balls, police and fireman balls… in fact, it was all balls! All were supplied with a grand buffet, most of them catered for by the local caterers Parsley's, of Red Lion Square. I remember well the centre displays of the very large, wonderful buffets, normally with a centrepiece of a full-size salmon laid out for serving.

Figure 24: Sheila and I at the Chamber of Trade ball in 1972. I am in the centre, wearing the medallion; Sheila is immediately to the left.

THE CHAMBER OF TRADE

The 1970s were a very busy time personally for me and my wife, Sheila, being involved not only in Duncomb's and Harrison & Dunn but also in the Chamber of Trade. Mr Dunn was a committee member of Stamford Chamber of Trade and in 1968 proposed that I join them. Much to my surprise, shortly after joining I was declared Vice President, supporting Mr Feetham, of Feetham's electrical shop, for two years. I was elected President the following year, and it took up a lot of my spare time as the Chamber was a very active group at this time, with different involvements with the Stamford Borough Council. A Stamford Development Committee was very important as it dealt with the development of Stamford in every aspect – industrial, residential, or social.

How lucky we were to have our own borough council, with our own local councillors deciding what would happen in our town, in one of the oldest boroughs in the country. Not like now, with the district and county council deciding what is best (or perhaps what is worst) for us from afar.

In 1972, as President of the Chamber of Trade, I reintroduced the Chamber of Trade's Trade Fair. We would take over the Assembly Rooms for a week and fill it with trade stands. There had not been one since 1963 (see *Figure 25*), although the last of great significance was in 1961, which was then the Stamford Borough's quincentenary year and when Lord Burghley himself was mayor. Our first restart of the Trade Fair was very successful. We were well supported by the local *Stamford Mercury* newspaper with a special pull-out Trade Fair supplement, and Lord Burghley and his wife opened the fair (see *Figure 26*). The fair had lots of competitions, including shop window displays, special deals, and ones that allowed the children to join in, such a treasure hunts. One such competition (which I remember playing as a child during the trade fairs held in my youth) was to spot the out-of-place items in shop windows, which different shops might place there on different days. I remember one day taking a box of

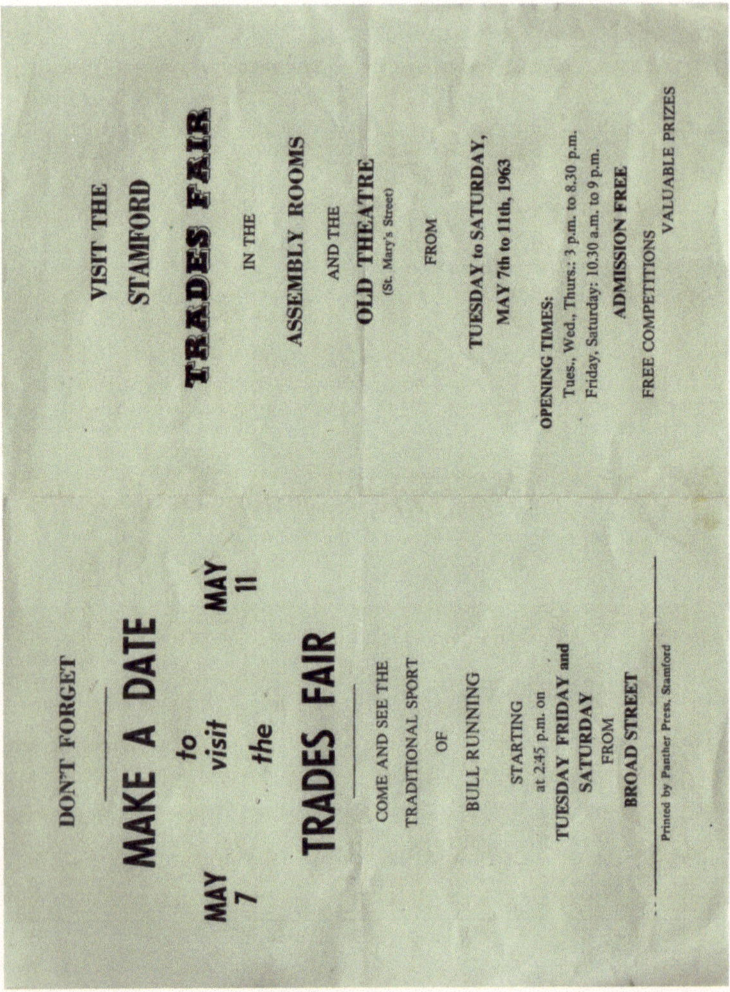

Figure 25: A flyer for the 1963 Stamford Trade Fair (image reproduced by kind permission of Spiegl Press Ltd).

screws to Nelsons (the butcher), who in turn gave me a pork pie. I then put the pork pie in Duncomb's shop window, and Nelsons put the box of screws in theirs.

This then became a regular local event which we organised every two or three years. Harrison & Dunn and Duncomb & Co. Ltd supported all the trade fairs, and kept me and my wife busy building and running our own trade stand. As the organisers, we had first choice for the site of our stall, and always had a stand in the main ballroom (see *Figure 27*). This proved very important at the Trade Fair of 1977… but more on that later. More photographs of the trade fairs can be seen in *Figures 28–30.*

Figure 26: Lord Burghley opens the 1972 Trade Fair. He is pictured third from the right; on the far left is the mayor's wife, Mrs Brodie, with her husband Mr Brodie, mayor, to the right; I am stood beside him, third from the left; Sheila is stood second from the right.

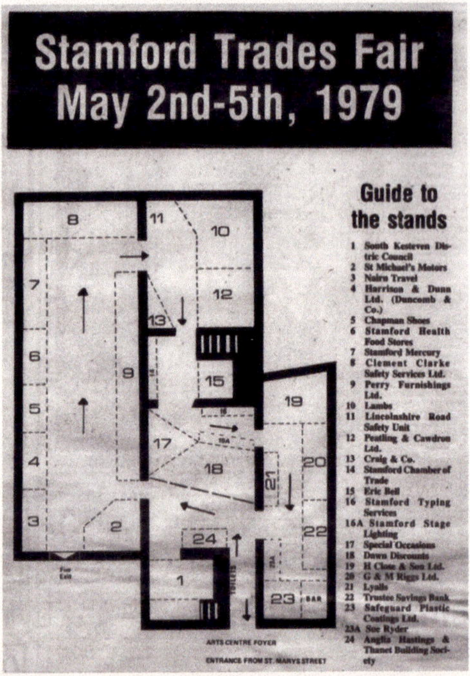

Stamford Trades Fair
May 2nd-5th, 1979

Guide to the stands

1 South Kesteven Distric Council
2 St Michael's Motors
3 Nairn Travel
4 Harrison & Dunn Ltd. (Duncomb & Co.)
5 Chapman Shoes
6 Stamford Health Food Stores
7 Stamford Mercury
8 Clement Clarke Safety Services Ltd.
9 Perry Furnishings Ltd.
10 Lambs
11 Lincolnshire Road Safety Unit
12 Peatling & Cawdron Ltd.
13 Craig & Co.
14 Stamford Chamber of Trade
15 Eric Bell
16 Stamford Typing Services
16A Stamford Stage Lighting
17 Special Occasions
18 Dawn Discounts
19 H Close & Son Ltd.
20 G & M Riggs Ltd.
21 Lyalls
22 Trustee Savings Bank
23 Safeguard Plastic Coatings Ltd.
23A Sue Ryder
24 Anglia Hastings & Thanet Building Society

ARTS CENTRE FOYER
ENTRANCE FROM ST. MARYS STREET

Figure 27: The floor plan of the 1979 Trade Fair, showing Harrison & Dunn and Duncomb & Co. Ltd in a prominent position.

Figure 28: The Duncomb & Co. Ltd stand at a Stamford Chamber of Trade Fair.

Figure 29: A picture of me manning a Duncomb & Co. Ltd stand.

Figure 30: A picture of me and my staff manning a Duncomb & Co. Ltd stand.

THE '70s ROLL ON

In 1973, Stamford (the same as other towns and cities) saw a very difficult time as we all suffered electric blackouts, with all power being switched off for periods of the day. This was as a result of the 1972 miners' strike depleting the reserves of coal at the power stations, with some places having a three-day week imposed on them by the government. At Duncomb's, I found some four or five paraffin pressure lamps in our old workshop (similar to the ones in the advert of the time shown in *Figure 31*). These I re-serviced, and they gave a wonderful light. These pressure lamps used paraffin under pressure, which you pumped up by hand. Once the stem got warm, paraffin ended up as gas using a gas mantle. So, with this

Figure 31†: A paraffin pressure lamp.

emergency lighting and a manual till, we never had to close. There were long queues outside the shop because we sold not only fuel, paraffin, and gas, but also candles; we had to restrict how many candles we sold to any one customer in order to be fair to all.

In 1974, the government reorganisation of district councils saw a very sad day for our historical town, as we lost control of our own town when the power was moved to South Kesteven District Council (SKDC), the offices of which were built in Grantham. Stamford, of course, had had one of the oldest borough councils in the country: over five hundred years old (a charter was granted to the corporation of Stamford in 1461).

The new district council wanted to take over our town hall and remove our valuable regalia (such as our civic jewellery, including a large ceremonial mace), but some of our local councillors dug their heels in. In fact, a new SKDC van turned up at the town hall to remove the regalia and take it to Grantham. The mayor's officer at that time, Tom Smith, was a retired police sergeant from Stamford, and he soon sent them back with their tail between their legs, with a definite 'no' and an ask for them to leave empty-handed at once. Good for you, Tom!

Actually, after nearly fifty years of SKDC closing most of Stamford's buildings, etc., and selling off all of its services, etc., the council are now beginning to hand back to Stamford one or two old buildings which have been of interest, and recently the Town Council have taken over some of the assets that the Stamford Borough Council had had all those years ago.

1974 saw another sad loss: the end of the Harrison & Dunn vans travelling around the local villages. With the increases in bus services and car ownership, the vans had become unnecessary, as most of our village customers were now making quite a few visits to Stamford. With a heavy heart, I here show the notice showing the withdrawing of the vans (*Figure 32*). The long-time travelling shop team of Reg Chambers and Arthur Thrift both came into the Harrison & Dunn shop, where they completed their working life (Harrison & Dunn have always been blessed with faithful and long-serving staff).

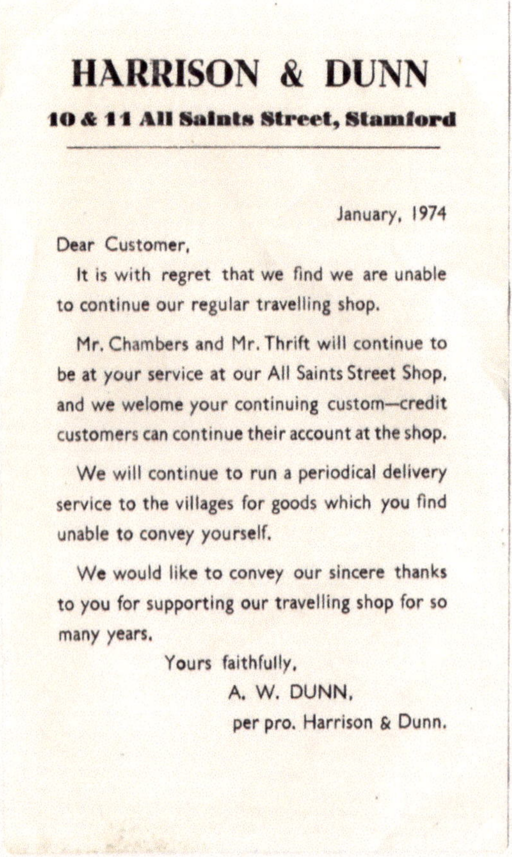

HARRISON & DUNN

10 & 11 All Saints Street, Stamford

January, 1974

Dear Customer,

It is with regret that we find we are unable to continue our regular travelling shop.

Mr. Chambers and Mr. Thrift will continue to be at your service at our All Saints Street Shop, and we welome your continuing custom—credit customers can continue their account at the shop.

We will continue to run a periodical delivery service to the villages for goods which you find unable to convey yourself.

We would like to convey our sincere thanks to you for supporting our travelling shop for so many years.

Yours faithfully,

A. W. DUNN,

per pro. Harrison & Dunn.

Figure 32: A notice of the withdrawal from service of the Harrison & Dunn travelling shops.

The other thing that happened in 1974 was the beginning of the pedestrianisation of the High Street, which introduced – and caused – a new decline in the trade of DIY and ironmongery on the High Street. As President of the Chamber of Commerce, I had to deal with organising the response and making the councils realise that – obviously – shops needed to be supplied, so you could not just close up the High Street without arranging for places and times for lorries to deliver stock, goods, and/or equipment.

1977 saw the Queen's Silver Jubilee year. The Chamber of Trade put on a Trade Fair, and the High Street was properly completed as a pedestrian precinct.

1972 had seen the building of the Stamford Arts Centre, which was organised and developed thanks to Lord Exeter and then-important local people Wilfred Woods, Miss Blackstone, and Mr Ireson. Sadly, the theatre that opened there in 1978 did not turn out for the local amateur dramatics societies. The local amateur dramatic societies were asked what would be ideal for them, theatre-wise, and they had asked for at least a three-hundred-seat theatre with an orchestra pit (and so on). This did not follow, and the smaller theatre (which we have there at the moment) was produced.

1976 saw my daughter Judith start working at the shop as a thirteen-year-old Saturday member of staff. This was followed by my son, Andrew, in 1979, and my daughter Karen in 1982. In 1979 to 1980, I was once again President of the Chamber of Trade, and continued the trade fairs, etc. This term included a major fight against on-street and car parking charges brought in by the new SKDC (as well as Lincolnshire County Council). This involved us holding several objection meetings and demonstrations. We also lobbied the SKDC offices in Grantham on the day of the council voting on this paid parking. We were pleased to stop the charges for on-street parking, which still remains free to this day.

CHAPTER 5

HARRISON & DUNN IN THE PRESENT

3 ALL SAINTS' STREET IS ACQUIRED

The 1977 Trade Fair was to celebrate one thousand years of Stamford's history. My trade stand was next to Lyall and Co., estate agents and valuers, so I got to know their Mr Clay very well as he was manning their stand. As the week went on, during conversations with the same, it was mentioned that they were trying to sell Bassendines' shop (which was the large general shop) and that they were surprised we had not put an offer in to purchase it. I said that the price of number 3 All Saints' Street (the address of Bassendines) was far more than we could afford, but I was informed at the Trade Fair that Mr Bassendine's family had now all retired and that they were fed up with the shop being empty (and having lots of trouble with the windows being broken, etc.), so it was suggested that I put in a very low offer to purchase it – and I, in fact, did. To my surprise, the next day a message came back from the Bassendines that they had accepted my offer. My partners at Harrison & Dunn were also surprised, but readily agreed that it would make a wonderful shop for Harrison & Dunn, being a larger and more convenient premises, and so once again, my building tools came out.

My wife undertook to paint all the inside of the new shop and the new pegboard sign. Sheila has always worked very hard for Harrison & Dunn, and yet her father, Mr Dunn, always treated her like a lackey. Her painting all of the shop is a fine example: instead of thanking her for her work, all Mr Dunn could do was complain about her asking for more and more Dulux white emulsion!

In 1978, when the renovated Bassendines shop was ready, Harrison & Dunn moved into it. We had our existing premises to sell (*Figures 33–34*), and it was at this time that Doctors Barker, Hibble, and Mitchell were looking to open up a new practice. We were able to sell our premises to them, marking the start of the Sheepmarket Surgery. This practised for many years, and it was a wonderful family doctors' surgery: caring, and very good. The practice later moved down to new

Figure 33: The Harrison & Dunn premises at 9, 10, and 11 All Saints' Street, 1975 (pencil drawing by A.G. Fitcher).

premises in the hospital grounds, where it is today; it is the same practice in name only.

FOR SALE BY PRIVATE TREATY

FREEHOLD COMMERCIAL PREMISES

9 10 & 11 All Saints Street,
Stamford, Lincolnshire.

LYALL & CO.

H. A. LYALL, F.R.I.C.S.
F. W. ASHER, F.R.I.C.S.
R. W. ASHER, A.R.I.C.S.
G. H. CLAY, B.Sc. (Est. Man.) A.R.I.C.S.

CHARTERED SURVEYORS, CHARTERED LAND AGENTS, AUCTIONEERS, ESTATE AGENTS & VALUERS

MARKET PLACE, BOURNE, LINCS. PE10 9NP.	50 HIGH STREET, STAMFORD, LINCS. PE9 2BD.	1 MAIDEN LANE, STAMFORD, LINCS. PE9 2BA.	9a WESTGATE, PETERBOROUGH, PE1 1PX.
Bourne 2431/2	Stamford 51934/5	Stamford 51934/5	Peterborough 61753 or 43271

Figure 34: Notice of sale for the Harrison & Dunn premises at 9, 10, and 11 All Saints' Street (image reproduced by kind permission of Golding Young).

THE CHILDREN FIND THEIR WAY

My daughter Judith decided that she did not want to stop at the shop, and when she left school she successfully pursued a business with the *Stamford Mercury* EMAP group, in their promotional side. My son, Andrew, decided to come and learn the ironmongery trade in 1983, when he left school and joined me in Duncomb's shop. He enjoyed the work, and was particularly interested in the locksmithing side of our business. I here include some of the thoughts that Andrew wrote down to be included in this book:

> I started to work for Harrison & Dunn's when I was thirteen, as a Saturday boy in their High Street shop, Duncomb & Co. Ltd, in 1979.
>
> One day, in the school holidays, I got woken up early, as one of the staff was ill and I had to go to work in the Bourne shop with Jim Dixon. He was in his seventies, and drove to Bourne in nine minutes! His accelerator foot hit the floor and he never braked once. On the way home, he pulled into the lay-by at Toft, got out, and said, 'Come on, boy, you drive home. I used to teach my boy like this.' I told him I was only fourteen and had no driving licence; he was quite put out that I didn't take him up on his offer. Later, in the same week, I had to go to Bourne with Reg Chambers. He was a lovely man who drove leisurely to Bourne in forty minutes. He used to hide a kettle in a box because Jim did not think it was right to use Mr Dunn's electricity to make a cup of tea.
>
> On Christmas Day, when I was aged fifteen, my grandad Albert Dunn sat down next to me on the sofa,

and his exact words to me were: 'Robert is leaving and there is a job going if you want it.' He paused and then added: 'Take it or leave it: you only get one chance.' In the 1980s, there was mass unemployment, so I thought I'd better take it. I was paid £34 a week (before tax); later that year, my grandad said he'd slipped up as he could have got me on a work experience scheme for £25 a week (that made me feel really valued). So, I left school on the Friday and started work on the Monday.

I worked at Duncomb's DIY, cutting wood and keys and selling ironmongery. I worked with John Pooley, who was Stamford's very own Arthur Daley (of *Minder* fame). He was always selling dodgy cars that broke down more often than not. He would say to me, 'I'm not here,' and then disappear; then I would have some bloke shouting at me because the car John had sold him and gone wrong. He could have had his own book for all the stories he told me. I became very good friends with John (he was in his sixties and I was sixteen). He would get me running around, pushing old cars, etc., for free like Terry (also from *Minder*). My first car came from him, and went to Seaton scrapyard before I ever even drove it.

Whilst working in Stamford (after I had passed my test), I had to drive Grandad home for his lunch one day. I was making deliveries just before, and knew he would not be happy as I was five minutes late picking him up. I have a very long fuse, but when I lose it, I lose it. When he started moaning at me, I went crazy, and told him what I thought of him with some very choice words (my mum would have got the soap out). He sat in the Bedford HA van (on a bit of foam, because there was only the driver's seat in the van as it was cheaper to buy like that) and I drove off like Lewis Hamilton. He was rolling all over the place, and when he eventually staggered out, I wheel-span off down the road. By the next day, I had calmed down, and all he said to me was, 'We won't have the wings, today.' After that, we never 'had words' again.

He (Albert) always reminded me of Captain Mainwaring (from *Dad's Army*) in his mannerisms. He started the business and came from very humble beginnings. Over the years, I spent many hours talking to him, and we were very close.

After I had worked in Duncomb's for three years, the shop was sold. During that period there was a big family meeting: the Bourne shop was losing money, and they were in two minds whether or not to keep it open (buying stock for two shops gave a better discount). I was asked to manage the Bourne shop at nineteen years old – I even got a company van (see *Figure 35*)!

The Bourne shop was like the *Open All Hours* store, with a till that had a handle, shelves like the 'four candles' sketch, and a long counter. In hindsight, it was a wonderful thing, and part of me wishes I had kept it as it was. But I was young, and 'new' was good at the time. All the B&Q superstores were killing independent hardware shops and many closed down as a result. The customers didn't really like the independent shops at the time, so it was sink or swim. I was the next generation of the family as the eldest grandson; I had big ideas, and modernised the shop, taking out all the old fixtures and fittings. I painted the shop interior white with red signage, and opened the windows so customers could see in. I did my market

Figure 35: Andrew Lee in his blue Harrison & Dunn van, when manager of the Bourne shop.

research, and ordered in more stock with improved offers: the turnover doubled within the first year. Grandad was pleased with my success, and would often call in for a royal visit to say hello (really, he was checking up on me).

I got the shop running so well it didn't really need me there. I was bored, but I had grand plans to open lots of small shops (the same as the Bourne shop) and I would run them all. I found a shop in Oakham, put a business plan together, and presented it to my dad and uncle. They said 'no', as they were happy with things as they were, so I said I would leave and do my own thing. I gave them a year's notice and decided to set up my own locksmithing firm, as I had passed my Master Locksmith exam.

My grandad never really forgave me for leaving (we never fell out or spoke about it). At the end of the day, I had worked at Harrison & Dunn for twelve years and was still only an employee. I was always told I would be a partner but I wasn't happy treading water. In life, you have to choose which path to walk down. As A.L. Locksmiths, I still work closely with Harrison & Dunn, and I get on well with my cousins who now run it.

DIFFICULT DECISIONS

Richard, Albert's son, was now happily running the Harrison & Dunn shop, and I Duncomb's (see Figure 36). Mr Dunn was past retirement age, yet was having difficulty accepting getting old and felt he could not let go of his part of the business. He decided to invite his cousin Mr Ray Dunn (who had been made redundant by Martin-Markham's engineering works, for which he had been the manager) to replace him in Harrison & Dunn when he retired. Not wishing to fall out with Mr Dunn, Richard and I said to give it a try, but he did not last for many weeks before Ray and Mr Dunn fell out and Ray left. Still mixed up with what to do about retirement, Mr Dunn tried another replacement in a travelling salesman he had known for many years, one who worked for our main, good-old wholesalers, Thomas Plant, of Birmingham. His name was Mr Tony Blow. He was a very nice, knowledgeable man, who Richard and I got on very well with, but I'm afraid the same thing happening with Mr Dunn as had happened to Ray: Mr Dunn could still not let go. So, Tony left our employ

Figure 36: A picture of me demonstrating stocktaking to one Stephanie, as part of a work experience placement (image reproduced by kind permission of the *Rutland and Stamford Mercury*).

and – I'm happy to say – opened with his son an ironmonger's shop of his own in Oundle, called Stu-Pots.

With the declining trade in Stamford High Street, it seemed to us that it was not practical to run two large shops in the same town. With the closing of the High Street into a precinct (and other factors), trade declined at Duncomb's. Now that Harrison & Dunn had a wonderful new shop in the Sheep Market, we decided to close the High Street shop in 1985/86.

When we had first moved into the old, large number 3 All Saints' Street, Harrison & Dunn took over the selling of children's clothes, toys, prams, and nursery goods from an old, well-established shop at number 10 Ironmonger Street, Woods J.L. (Mrs Woods, who ran it, had retired) (see *Figure 37*). This department filled the shop, and was run by my wife,

Sheila. When Duncomb's moved into Harrison & Dunn, we decided to remove the trade taken on from Woods J.L.'s so that there would be room for the DIY, the timber, and the kitchen, bedroom, and bathroom design and fitting service which I had built up in the High Street. Most of my staff and I were relocated to the Harrison & Dunn shop; my son moved to our Bourne shop. My youngest daughter, Karen, who had been working with us as a Saturday girl, moved on to pursue a career in dental nursing.

After so many years of trading and all the work I had been involved in with Duncomb's, it was a very sad time for

Figure 37: Advert showing the trade of Woods J.L. at Harrison & Dunn, 1979 (image reproduced by kind permission of the *Rutland and Stamford Mercury*).

me. The selling off was very painful, and I must say I shed quite a few tears.

Mr Dunn, again, could not accept getting old, and now with only one shop to manage (which Richard and I would run together) we persuaded him to carry on doing office work for us, which he did right up to just before his death in 2005.

So, the 1980s and 1990s continued to be very successful for Harrison & Dunn – Stamford and Bourne (see *Figure 38*). I very much enjoyed working alongside my wife, Sheila, and brother-in-law, Richard. Andrew came forward to Richard

Figure 38: A picture of me decorating Harrison & Dunn for the 50th anniversary of VJ Day, 1995 (image reproduced by kind permission of the *Rutland and Stamford Mercury*)

and me with a proposal to develop our business and expand, a proposal that involved many more shops being opened (starting in Oakham and carrying on from there). Richard and I, at the age we were and the easy life we seemed to then have, did not feel like all the work it involved to take up his plan. I often wonder now where Harrison & Dunn would be if we had taken up Andrew's plan. Andrew was naturally disappointed, and soon after left Harrison & Dunn to set up his own business as a locksmith, which he had spent many years learning and was by then a Master Locksmith. He continues with his trade as A.L. Locksmiths to this day.

SHEILA AND I RETIRE

In 1991, the local people who were running the Arts Centre found that they could not continue doing so, so it was taken over by SKDC for the council to run. In the same year, there was a sad day for business in Stamford when the famous engineering firm Blackstone's closed: a great loss to the town. This was the start of a decline of Stamford as a well-known engineering town.

As the new millennium approached, and my own and Sheila's retirement age, I became involved in a project to take over the Stamford Corn Exchange and turn it into a full-time theatre. The local amateur groups still needed a theatre of considerable size, with an orchestra pit and enough seats. If the Arts Centre theatre had been constructed as the local groups had asked, this project would not have been necessary.

My wife, Sheila, was a bit reluctant to retire, but eventually agreed, and we both retired from our Harrison & Dunn in 2005 (see *Figure 39*). We have had together a wonderful retirement of nineteen years, which has been nineteen years of a new career for me as a managing trustee of a registered charity, of building and running a full-time theatre; but here lies another story.

Harrison & Dunn continue to trade very successfully as traditional ironmongers in Stamford and Bourne. It still has many of the same loyal and long-serving staff, with Christine and Helen both completing over fifty years' service. It is still in the ownership of and run by my nephews, Richard's sons David and John, with Richard still working part-time (a real chip off the old block) (see *Figure 40*).

Good luck to it, and long may it run, with its traditional:

'Good morning, sir or madam, are you being served? Can we help you?'

Figure 39: Retirement. A picture of Sheila and me, soon after retiring in 2005.

Figure 40: The staff of Harrison & Dunn in 2010, on the shop's 80th anniversary. David Dunn is pictured on the far left; John Dunn is second from the right; and Richard Dunn is on the far right.

ABOUT THE AUTHOR

Michael Lee was born in Stamford, Lincolnshire, in March 1940. He grew up in the town (living on Lambeth Walk), and in 1955 became an apprentice carpenter for the local Burghley Estate. After completing his apprenticeship, Lee worked in the building and civil engineering trade, before becoming a partner in Harrison & Dunn in 1968. Lee went on to be extremely active in the local Chamber of Trade, twice serving as President.

Outside of his work as a carpenter and ironmonger, Lee was an established performer in local amateur dramatics for over sixty years. He was a talented comedic performer, and appeared regularly in annual pantomimes. In the 2000s, he led the conversion of the historic Stamford Corn Exchange into a dedicated theatre, and his retirement was spent serving as a trustee of the Corn Exchange Theatre Company.

Michael Lee died in Stamford in 2024.